Lee Sidney

A POEM OR TWO FROM ME TO YOU

AUSTIN MACAULEY PUBLISHERS
LONDON * CAMBRIDGE * NEW YORK * SHARJAH

Copyright © Lee Sidney Fletcher 2025

The right of Lee Sidney Fletcher to be identified as author of this work has been asserted by the author in accordance with sections 77 and 78 of the Copyright, Designs and Patents Act 1988.

All rights reserved. No part of this publication may be reproduced, stored in a retrieval system, or transmitted in any form or by any means, electronic, mechanical, photocopying, recording, or otherwise, without the prior permission of the publishers.

Any person who commits any unauthorised act in relation to this publication may be liable to criminal prosecution and civil claims for damages.

A CIP catalogue record for this title is available from the British Library.

ISBN 9781528989152 (Paperback)
ISBN 9781528989169 (Hardback)
ISBN 9781528989176 (ePub e-book)

www.austinmacauley.com

First Published 2025
Austin Macauley Publishers Ltd®
1 Canada Square
Canary Wharf
London
E14 5AA

Two Geese and a Gander

Two geese and a gander
On the veranda
Watching their goslings play
All day long, they eat grass
And time will pass – eating plenty of grass
A handful of mixed corn at the close of day
Put them in a good big shed
With plenty of shavings and hay
And in the morning they both might lay
A nice big egg to put on display
Then cook one at midday
Fry it well and fry it slow
A nice big yolk for you to dip your bread into
As the goslings grow, winter will near
And after that it will be new year.

Two Geese and a Gander part 2

Two geese and a gander
On the veranda
Watching their goslings play
Give them plenty of straw to lie on
And they will surely lay
A nice, big egg for dinner or tea
Oh what a sight to see!
A nice strong, safe shed at night
Away from foxes eyes they be
You don't need a lawn mower
Geese will keep the grass much lower.

Their head and necks will be up and down
For most of the day
Until their crops are full
And then a drink and a dip in their pool
To help keep their feathers clean
When dusk brings skies of grey
A handful of mixed corn
Then lock them safely away
At the end of the day – and early next day
The geese will surely lay

They will lay in a hole in the shavings and straw
And cover them over, out of sight
So when you let them out the next day
Run your fingers through the shavings and straw
Somewhere, hidden, on the shed floor
Two or three eggs
Turn a dinner for the poor
Into a feast for a king.

Kangaroo

One kangaroo said,
"I can jump further and faster than any of you
So follow me if that's all you lot can do
Follow the biggest and best kangaroo
Follow me do
All you other kangaroos."

Superman planet

Left side blue side is your modern superman blue vegetarian side
The way to the future planet
Smoke free and a way forward
Better world for everyone

Right side red side carnivore side
With the old ways and smoke
Smoking chimneys the old fashioned way

Two Geese And A Gander Part 3

Two geese and a gander
On the veranda
Watching their goslings play
Give them plenty of straw to lie on
And they will surely lay
A big, white egg you can put on display
And then you can eat it one day
For breakfast or tea
It is a real treat

Buzzards Fly part 1

Buzzard soaring to and fro
Looking everywhere as he goes
Looking in every nook and cranny
Down below
Till something catches his eye
He swoops down from the sky
Way up high to way down low
He grabs his prey and carries it away
Finds his cliff and eats it so
Buzzards Fly Part 3

Buzzards Fly Part 2

The buzzards fly way up in the sky
Soaring to and fro
Up and down, looking for a meal
He soars down low
As something's caught his eye
There he's seen
In the grassy green
A rabbit sitting there
Beware rabbit, beware!
The buzzard has seen you down there
The buzzard swept down low
Took the rabbit in his talons
Sharp as you know

Buzzards Fly Part 3

In the air, way up high...
Is where the handsome buzzards fly
Head held turned and wings spread wide
Around and around he flies
Looking sharp to roost before it gets dark
He will sit tight on his eggs
On some nearby stoney ledge
Then the parents will swoop over at dawn
So one bird will fly up high
Soaring up in the sky
Watching down below
For something to move or show
Then he will get the prey in his sights
He will swoop down before his prey will know
Held tight in deadly sharp talons
Then pinned down to the ground
And head bitten off and torn apart
Then the male bird will take the prey
Back to the stoney crest and the nest
And feed the young, one and all
Three or four young they will have
In the ledge of their nursery bed
Without the preys head
The body is fed to the biggest and strongest young
And they might be the only one to survive
To reach adulthood and carry on
As their parents have done
Through the millennia

Rabbits

Two little rabbits sat near a hole
Eating the nice green grass
For life is good when you are young
And starting out in life
Mum and dad keep all the worries and trouble away
Until you are trapped
An have to get out of danger one day
Or hide away
When danger approaches
And until it goes away
Living out in the field
In the thickets and grass
Lie life slow or live life fast
And try to make your life last
Hiding from dogs and birds of prey
Just so you live another day
In May

Another Day

One day you will get up and start another day
But before you get up
Have a think
About what you want to achieve today
That will help you start the day
And you will have a better day
Thinking of what you will do today
So have a wonderful day today
And may god go with you on this day
Anyway…enjoy each day

Morning Dew

The morning dew glistens
In the early morning sun
After night is done
And the day has begun
Glistening teardrops they might be
From shuddery cold nights
As cold they may be
For the cold of the night is right
There in sight
But after the sun does rise up
All the morning dew drops will dry up

And when the clock hands reach 11am
All will be dry and warm once again
On a warm summer's day
There might be a glassy haze
Just up in the summer skies
And then the cold summer nights
Will create mist
Then again morning dew
And the new day starts

Christmas Part 2

Christmas comes but once a year
Filling the land with love and cheer
So do not fear
Give a beer
Oh what a wonderful time of year
Christmas – when it's here
Christmas

Eagles Fly

Eagles fly and soar in the summer breeze
Up above the mountains and trees
In the summer breeze
The rabbits run down below
But the rabbits are really far too slow
When the eagles swoop down
To catch their prey
Then fly to a ledge to eat it
After, he soars back up into the summer breeze
Up above the mountain and trees
In the summer breeze

Pollution

Pollution is no solution
To mother earth's future
Know now it is slowing how
Progression in time down is throwing
Us out of ur main course
For mankind is forever progressing
Building a better foundation
For life for the human race
But problem pollution is slowing us down
In one of the worse ways possible
Burning coals and all the fossil fuels
Should be banned
In the 21st century they should be made
A thing of the past and forgotten
We should use ways that are modern
For our heating and lighting
Fast flowing rivers for electric
Wind turbines can only protect
The resources we have left
More wind turbines collecting
And cleaning up the atmosphere
Cleaning up everything
For this modern way – the only way
Forward, and for generations to come
To enjoy Mother Earth
For the centuries to come
Think less about money
Be more environmentally friendly
Now and for always
For the future of the human race
And for mankind

Pigs

Two little pigs kept in a pen
Eating and drinking as much as they can
"Soon I'll be fat" one of them said
Then the farmer will chop off my head
He'll gut me and clean me
Then feed me at tea
To all of his hungry family

Sheep

Two sheep eating grass
The farmer came up had shot one dead
He fed it to his family instead
Kids will grow well on lamb meat
They didn't go hungry with all the lamb meat to eat

Sheep Part 2

Two little sheep eating down grass
One said to the other,
"I'll eat my grass down fast!"
The other sheep said, "Eat it down slow
Or you'll grow too fast
Then you'll be off for the farmers dinner
He'll eat you all up
Until you are gone
Then you won't be eating this grass
So don't eat the grass too fast."

Two Little Girls

Two little girls playing on a swing
One said to the other
"When I grow up I'm going to sing
I'll sing through the night
Until I get it right
Then I'll make lots of money
Singing songs well and right
Until the dawn of morning comes-
What will you do?"
As the other girl pushed her gently so
In the sunny day of summers years ago
Make it last.

Otter

One otter caught himself a fish
Eating it down, he said, "It's my favourite dish"
Another Otter said, "Give me some of your fish
Because fish is my favourite dish."
The other otter said,
"It's all in your head, this is my fish," he said
"And you're off your head
If you think I'll give you my fish,"
The first Otter said.

Tomorrow In The Sun

Tomorrow is just another day
Always look at it that way
Slowly open your eyes and see
The sunlight blazing through the curtains
Shut tight so
But the morning sun still shines through
For morning is here
It is another day
Another day has begun
Early enough to have some fun
Run around in the sun
All day long running around
Playing games with all your friends
Endless days playing in the sun
All day long having fun
While the sun lasts...
Enjoy!

Live life as best as you know
Live it as good as you know
Live it for the people you know
Look after the family and friends you know
For life is shorter than you know
Go forward in life helping those you know
Find a good woman and love her so
Have kids and raise a family as best as you know
Look after the shell you live in
And your shell will look after you
Through your life
Life is not about drinking every day
Or about abusing your shell in messy ways
But helping others who you know
Will go a long way
Love people and try to help others around you

And they will help you back
While your shell is still growing
So are you, from life's mysteries
As you go, now and then
Think about your life
About where you are going
Or where you want to be
Find some good company
Look after your shell as it grows and ages

Your mind will get stronger
You may learn to cut corners For the better
For a better life ahead
Don't drink every day away
Find two nights a week and go have a drink
With age comes wisdom and skills
Then when you are old you are 6 again
Until you die and leave your shell behind
Your spirit is reborn into the afterlife
Young, and very happy.

Be Next To Me

I'm your type so you said
Looking at you I would say the same
For you're a cracker
Let's get together forever
From Lee

You look nice, I can see
But you would look better next to me
With your long black hair
You look a gem
With your long legs
They will look so fine
Next to mine
Together we will be a picture
You and me

Puv The Griys Peg The Horses

Mancey went to puv the griys all
I went to peg the horses all
Upon the parney side
Upon the riverside
Up jumped an old mush
Up jumped an old man
Mancey had to deck him
PUNCH
Mancey did deck him
I had to punch him I've got to go Mancey
Go tell Muchmans
That the police are coming
Mancey got to go, I've got to tell now!

Night

The moon has filled the heavenly sky
The stars are shining
Oh so bright
The tawny owl hunting cry
The fox cry in the distance
He is hunting to and fro
From rabbit shed to duck shed
Checking if the doors are all locked...
If just one is open
He will go in
And kill them all one by one
Pull their heads off until they are all dead
Then he will take all he can carry
With him off into the night...
Out of sight, into
The night

Seasons

November, December, January
The winter months are bitter cold
At the lake, and the ducks, geese and swans
Are foraging for food
The water iced over and the snow around
Some people feed the waterfowl
Bread and corn they've brought from town
The coots, moorhens and great-crested grebes
Are all pecking around
February, March and April
Spring is here
Then it soon gets warm
Time for everything to grow
Grass, bulbs, and flowers do well
The water fowl can start to feed again
In the water and the reeds
May, June, July
The summer months
The waterfowl all have their young
August, September, October
The summer fades away
The autumn days are here again
Then its soon winter
So the cycle continues
In the story of the year on the lake.

Ducks And A Drake

Four Ducks and a Drake
Floating on a lake, big mistake
If the hunters come in the morning
With their gun
Best make haste and fly away
To somewhere special and safe.

Billy Goat

A big goat sitting on a hill
Silly Bill, sitting on a hill
You ought to come down
And get your fill
Of grass from the meadow
Below, instead on that hill
Silly Bill, king of that hill

Tigers

Two tigers fighting
They were like lightning
Swishing their paws
And claws about
They were ferocious
Biting and clawing each other
Glad I'm not there
Because of tigers
They must be somewhere

Grandad

Grandad you're not mad
You're my dad's dad
And my granddad
Grandad

Blonde 2

A big leggy blonde came along
And gave us a song
It didn't take long, the song
And then she went along
On her way
She might come back another day
In May

Two Geese and A Gander 4

Two geese and a gander
On the veranda
Watching their goslings play
Give them plenty of shavings and straw to lie on
And they will surely lay
A big white egg to put on display
For all the people to see
Then you can eat it for
Breakfast dinner or tea
Yummy yummy yummy

Winter Night

Smoggy winter is here
For it is that time of year
smoggy winter is on the hill
But smog in the air
Is a wonderful sight
Helps in the morning
To get things right
It helps me sleep well at night
Living here on the Derbyshire hills
Fulfills your life and makes you live
A wonderful life
I wouldn't live anywhere else
so I think I've got it right
Living in the hills
1 sleep well at night
Each and every night

When I Was A Lad

When I was a lad
As big as me dad
I used to ride a Pony
I got a stick and tittled his?
And made him shit macaroni

Faye

Oh Faye
Come round today and make my
day In every way
Make my day special and say
I love you Walt
And I won't bolt, I'm here to stay
Says Faye
For you're the best Walt, in every way
I'm with Faye today and forever more
You're walty bear with no hair

The First Day

The first day I met you
1 knew 1 would never forget you
So come on be mine
Until the end of time
And we will sing our sweet rhyme
Together in paradise, you and me
For all time our mind would fly
Around the heavenly sky
Up there in paradise
Forever more – with you dear

Early One Morning

Early one morning my dad said to me,
"Son, come on son, to the horse fair with me."
We set off in the morning
At the breaking of day
As we travelled we passed
Travelling people as they made their journey
was saw draught horses, race horses, cobs and hunters
Even smaller ponies, but they were few
On the way to Appleby horse fair
In Cumbria near the lakes and mountains

Tom Cats

Not last night, the night before
There came three tom cats to my door
One with a fiddle
One with a bow
And one with a plant pot
On his toe!!

Hanna

There once was a girl called Hanna
Who always wanted a peahanno
Her mother said no and brought her a pow
And said now have a
Peahanna

Do Not Fear

Oh Kezia do not fear, we are here
Shining high in the heavenly sky
Oh we are the leaders of the light
But we only come out at night
Do not fret, you will see
The universe belongs to every creed
And bread aplenty for hungry mouths to feed

We will sow seed in a furrow
That will be good tomorrow
Living well, make this world more heavenly
For there are much better things than money or greed
Where all the hungry mouths can eat around the world
Our way will grow
And forward in time we will go

And a better place earth will be
And maybe some good friends from another galaxy
Just like mankind
Live with open heart and open hands
One much more advanced than us
And they will teach us all their ways for peace on earth
And centuries will go by
And the human race will learn to fly
Way way up there in the sky
The universe and sky –
Bye

The Midnight Fox

Trippety trot goes the midnight fox
Looking for a poultry shed unlocked
In he will creep
While the hens are fast asleep
And one by one he will pull
All their heads...
OFF!!!!!

Two Little Boys

Two little boys walking to school one day
One said to the other,
"When I grow up I'll be nobody's fool
I'll get a diploma
I'll get a degree
And 1 will rule this county."

He'll pile them high all together
And when they're all dead
He'll carry some off into the night
He will travel all night
Looking for a door unlocked
A hen house, duck shed or pigeon coop
Anything will be nice to eat
While you are fast asleep
Across the countryside he will travel
Ten miles or more every night
Just waiting for you to forget or slip up
One night.

Wooden tit

Woodentit woodentit
Woodentit be funny
If a cow had a wooden tit
Woodentit be funny

Luck at the back

Hens usually lay, an egg a day
So, me and you can have an egg, or two
They lay for eight months a year
Hen go into malt, so do not fear
They will lay another 8 months next year
Keep them two or three years
Then get rid, then to auction and bid
For some more.

Valentine Poem

Black is white and white is black
I will hold you close all night
Beneath the sheets we will be
A perfect couple, you and me
Because we got the rest of our lives
Live together you and me
What perfect harmony!

Let's share our lives you and me
For we will be together for eternity
Every year will be or anniversary
So, marry me
And you will see

I will always make time for thee
Together in perfect harmony
Our love will grow way up high
Up into the heavenly sky
Way up where the stars do shine
You be mine, sweet valentine?

Poems for Alison

Oh Alison, your eyes are so fine like diamonds
At the side of mine, yours shine so fine
Be forever mine – Lee

Oh Alison, your eyes are so nice
Cool like ice, and just for that I want a slice
So just be nice, Ally – Lee

Oh Alison, you're so fine I think of you all the time
So just be mine until the end of time?
Sweet Ally love – Lee

Oh Alison, if only I could make you mine
Until the end of time, that would be fine
So fine real fine, babe – Lee

Oh Alison, to go on a date with you
Would make all my dreams come true
So, come on babe, say you will
And that will do, Ally – Lee

Oh Alison, now I have met you
I can never forget you
But I am so glad I met you
Yours forever – Lee

Oh Alison, in your heart I want to be
We could make it, you and me
I know it for sure Ally – Lee

So please end my misery
And come on a date with me to the cinema or the sea
We could be magic together you and me – Lee

Oh Alison, come to Blackpool with me
Lee and Alison by the sea
then back to Ripley
You and me – Lee

Oh Alison, sit down on my knee
And we will have a cup of tea
Made by gypsy Lee
And talk about the future
For us Ally – Lee

Oh Alison, you're my little dove
my shining light
Sign from above
My sweet little dove
With love – Lee

Oh Alison to your good looks
Not money could compare
Your beautiful long, dark hair
Excuse me if I stop and stare
I'd follow you anywhere – Lee

Oh Alison, do you like the weather
It's time we got together babe
You're in my heart every day
Please say you'll stay with me, forever
Sweet Ally – Lee

Oh Alison, it fills me full of cheer knowing you are near
So, we will have to have a beer
I'll drink to that
My dear- Lee

Oh Alison, you're just like a good wine
So mature and real fine
I wish you were mine, until the end of time
Be mine sweet Ally – Lee

Oh Alison, you're the one for me
Give me a try and you will see
We will make a lovely couple, you and me
Say yes Ally – Lee

No better love you will see
If you belonged to me, and I belonged to thee
Yours forever – Lee

Suzy

Suzy Suzy, Don't be so choosey and come and sit on my knee Suzy Suzy.

Suzy Suzy was just having a little snoozy wasn't you Suzy?

The shop keeper said to the customer, Sir do you want a bag? And the customer said 'I've just got rid of one of those and she isn't coming back'

Geraldine

Geraldine don't you be so mean Geraldine and come and be my beauty queen Geraldine.

Geraldine come and be my beauty queen Geraldine the best-looking woman I've ever seen Geraldine.

Annette

Annette Annette don't do anything you will regret, Annette my pet.

Lesseyann

She is called Lesseyann not lesbian, and she pushes a pram does Lesseyann.

Faye

Ho Faye come around today and we will just lie there anyway my beautiful Faye today Faye.

Maria

Maria be mine and til the end of time and we will have a sip of wine Ho my sweet Mary

Penny

Penny Penny don't be so merry Penny if you haven't got any left Penny the reason is because you are already so merry Penny, so let Penny be merry Penny.

Catlean

Ho Catlean you are always so clean Catlean. And you make a nice, gorgeous scene. Ho my sweet Catlean, Catlean.

Brenda

Brenda let's go on a bender Brenda. We can always borrow a pound or two. Just because it's you. Ho Dear Brenda.

Joey

Ho Joey you are always so gowe Joey so let's have a cup of tea, do you like it sweet and strong? A cuppa won't take long. Do you like your tea strong?

Linda

Linda why are you always so slender and tall Linda? People will always remember you my dear Linda.

Lorraine

Ho Lorraine lets go on a train, my dear sweetest Lorraine, it's not going to rain my Lorraine. We will soon be on the train Lorraine, I've just unlocked the drain Lorraine.

Brenden

Brenden go on to the next one Brenden, go down the country roads to London Brendon. You will soon get to the end road Brendon.

Nata Lie

Ho Nata Lie Dawson you are so good to me.
How love will grow on forever you see?
And we will make history, my little chickadee.
My Nata Lie and me Lee xxx

Nata Lie and Lee beside the sea Ho let it be.
An awesome sight to see,
Nata Lie and Lee beside the sea,
my dearest Nata Lie, just you wait and see Nata Lie and Lee beside the sea Nata Lie. Xx

Ho Nata Lie you are that good looking to me.
And to me you are so awesome to see.
And it helps that you belong to me, my dear Nata Lie x

Nata Lie, it freezes me because you are so great to see.
I would spend the rest of my life with you my little cockatoo.
I love you x Natalee xxx

Ode to a stranger

Oh, dear lady of who I don't know
I could think of a hundred reasons
Why I love you so
And a hundred reasons more
Just why I've got to know you
So, come on dear lady
Do you want to know
Who we both are, dear lady?

Jenna

Oh Jenna, you're quite a head turner
Stunning to see out on a Saturday night
I look at you with delight
You look and dress just right
Sometimes I say
"Are you alright?"
Dancing away on a Saturday night.

Although I adored you
From the first time I saw you
I can't say I know you
But if things were different
I would get to know you
Do you want to know me?
When you make up your mind
I will know then, if my love
I shall give to you also

Christmas

Christmas comes but once a year
And it fills everyone full of cheer
Some may have a beer
Others go to church to sing with cheer
And great joy...
A day to have a nice dinner
To give presents to each other
One and all for the kids
To have a good time
To watch them smile
To hear them laugh and feel good

Winter Snow

When all the autumn mud has gone away
When the blanket of winter snow covers the land
Snow – white, clean and bright
Everything is delightfully nice
Looking at the warm blanket of snow
It covers everywhere
Christmas day is approaching close
The sound of bells chimes in our towns and cities

Nursery rhymes and carols chime
For it is Christmas time!
A time for giving and receiving
Presents and best wishes
For all and to all mankind
Then the snow finally melts away
The green grass, soil and roads greet you again
Christmas time...

Living Life

Living life can be a strain
And can be filled with heartache and pain
And then we pick ourselves up
And start again
Back on track down the road of life
Once again midway through
We might stop
And take a look at what we've got
And have achieved from time to time
We do this and reminisce
At the troubled time
We wouldn't have missed
Because these are the times
That have made us strong
Along life's wonderful road
Some might give up and die
Others grow strong as they mature
And get better at living life to the full
Learning lessons as they go
Down life's long long road
Making new friends as they go
And till the end we must go
Living life to its full middle age
Life is just being time to remain
And start again
Some more kids
And a new future
Together with someone new
You use your head more as you grow
Live for a century if you can
Then when you're old
And life's nearly done
You will be six years old again
Before you die

And then when you die
Your spirit will be born
Into the afterlife
After living life
To the full

Two Dogs

Two dogs having a fight
One said, "Alright?"
The other dog said,
"I'm looking for your brother
I'm going to give him another
I'll be the best dog around
One of a kind
So keep that in mind."

Helping People Today

Helping others who do rely on you
Will make a lot more things come true

So enjoy life to the full
And make somebody's day
In every way, you can
And they will help you one day
On you day helping
Is the only way
Helping people on their way
Help someone today

Autumn Trees

The leaves are falling off the trees
Autumn is here again
The rain falls Autumn is here again
But when the autumn mud has gone away
Winter will be on its way
Snow white over the ground
Will be a pretty sight for all to see
Christmas day will soon be here
All the kids will give a cheer
A good time of year
When winter is here

Autumn to Winter

When the autumn mud has gone away
That's when the winter does set in
The ground will be covered with white over
A wonderful sight to see
All snow white – a perfect sight
The gardens look the same
As children play in the snow
On their sledges they will go
Up and down the hillside
In the snow
Christmas day will soon be here
They all know...

Blonde

A tall blonde came along
She sang a song
It took quite long
But she did nothing wrong
But sang a song

Christmas Song

Ho Christmas time is here
So everyone do not fear
Ho Christmas time is here
In the woods you'll find a tree
A Fir tree evergreen
Nice and bright
Christmas time, that's the sign
Of Christmas

Christmas

After the autumn mud is covered up with
The first blanketing of snow on the ground
It all looks real clean
Ripley town is such a sight
With all the streets shining so
Because they are all covered over
With fresh and falling snow
Christmas time it soon will be
A better time for you and me
And near Christmas up goes the tree
Big presents and little presents
For all to see
A present for everyone in the family
For Christmas morning
Surprise for all and a time to make merry!

Winter (Christmas)

When winter comes around
At that time of year
The whole atmosphere
Is filled with joy and cheer
Christmas time of year
Have a beer
With your mates
Buying presents that just can't wait
For all the girls and boys
Plenty of books and toys
Cooking big fat Turkeys for
Christmas dinner
Brushing the snow away
To clear the path
Or someone might slip and fall down flat
And we can't have that
At winter time
That special time of year – Christmas

Merry Christmas

Merry Christmas everyone
Seasonal fun and happiness
To everyone
Come join in the seasons fun
Presents and parties for everyone
Come join in on the fun

Winter Snow

When all the Autumn mud is gone away
And winters snow white blanket covers the land
Snow white and clean and bright
Everything's nice and delightful
To see the warm blanket of snow
Covers everywhere
For Christmas day
Is approaching close

The sound of bells cover our towns and cities
Nursery rhymes and carols chime
For it is
Christmas time
A time for giving and receiving
Presents and best wishes
For all and to all mankind
Then the snow does melt away
And you see
Green grass and roads and soil again
Christmas times